Margaritas and Redfish

Margaritas and Redfish

Ken Hada

LAMAR UNIVERSITY *press*

ISBN: 978-0-9850838-6-1
Library of Congress Control Number: 2013954490

Cover paintings: Duane Hada, "Tailing Redfish"
Book Design: Carol Weishampel
Manufactured in the United States

Lamar University Press
Beaumont, Texas

Acknowledgments

Some poems in this collection first appeared in the following journals and anthologies, some in slightly different arrangements. The author thanks the editors of these publications:

adaHub
California Quarterly
Crosstimbers
Desert Candle
di-verse-city
Enigmatist
Illya's Honey
Licking River Review
Meridian Anthology of Contemporary Poetry
Mountain High: a poetry and prose anthology
Naugatuck River Review
Oklahoma Today
Redlionsquare.com
Red River Review
San Pedro River Review
Sand, Sea and Sail: a poetry and prose anthology
Sugar Mule
This Land: Relevant Readings Regarding Oklahoma
Write Choice Journal

I am especially grateful to Susan Gardner for her significant insight concerning this manuscript. I am also grateful to my writing friends Joshua Grasso, Rayshell Clapper and Jessica Isaacs for their careful reading and encouragement during the process of these poems.

I am grateful to the Administration and Faculty Research and Professional Development Committee at East Central University, Ada, Oklahoma whose grant provided considerable time toward the completion of this project.

Poetry from Lamar University Press:

Alan Berecka, *With Our Baggage*
David Bowles, *Flower, Song, Dance*: Aztec *and Mayan*
       Poetry (a new translation)
Jerry Bradley, *Crownfeathers and Effigies*
Jeffrey DeLotto, *Voices Writ in Sand*
Mimi Ferebee, *Wildfires and Atmospheric Memories*
Michelle Hartman, *Disenchanted and Disgruntled*
Janet McCann, *The Crone at the Casino*
Erin Murphy, *Ancilla*
Dave Oliphant, *The Pilgrimage, Selected Poems: 1962-2012*
Carol Reposa, *Underground Musicians*

For information on these and other Lamar University Press books go to
    www.LamarUniversityPress.Org

Other Books by Ken Hada

The Way of the Wind
Spare Parts
The River White

For more information about Ken Hada's writing go to
http://kenhada.org/

for Taylor

CONTENTS

she is leaving me
for the sun
she may be disappointed
when she discovers
that we are twins

Saul Williams

Meditation

To what landscapes shall we give ourselves:

Deserts vast, overwhelming
where stars trump even the brightest hopes

Gulf coasts where silver sand trout
surf the bordering sun

Ozark streams at sunset

Crosstimber and prairie extending us beyond
like Sand Cranes in night flight

Lodgepole pines silent above us

the Pacific where love cuts like coral
fatal palms swaying, weeping?

Let these places serve notice
that hope comes with warning,
let them witness: I was there
with canoe and tent, with rod and reel

I was there
and others accompanied us
others knew us
where grace empties
into a delta and salvation
belongs to a congregation of krill
loitering, unsuspecting as a wave.

Blue River Cedars

Straight rough-
bark stoics
unmoved by wind
or birds

rise to stars.
Moonglow
across trunks
unswayed

watch over
our tent pitched
in the temple
of silence.

Where Winter Has Been

In a green field of new clover
eternal in its infancy
purple and white crocus point upward
to a bluebird sky, tiny, fragile
yet strong for their effort

rising among dead brown briars
muted cedar and twisted scrub oak
broken limbs fallen from cottonwoods
scattered across an emerging world
where winter has been.

Sundown on the Blue River

White sun lingers above falls
cascading ancient rock

    silver leafless sycamores
    rusty oaks
    yellow grass, green cedar.

Find the trail
take the long way back.

Drive home
to a dark neighborhood.

Light a candle.

Hear an anxious pup
    across the street
bark incessant cries
    being left alone.

Canoeing

Our love a swirling river,
my oar

       dripping
       marking new patterns

pull us through deeper pools

       peaking rhythms

plunge into swift rapids

       spraying glee.

Hold tight.
Paddle hard.

Float to bliss beyond doubt.

Land softly
on sun-swept sand.

Morning Brew

Tin coffee pot

      steams

in campfire, sleep

      lingers

numb in crisp air
loose flannel shirts.

Rousing aroma

      bubbles

in coals stirred
from night-fire

      a bird above us
      water galloping

steaming breaths

      wait—eyes

fixed on fire.

Into Light

From shadows
we leave camp
beneath pine and hemlock
egress onto the lake

paddle softly
unable to see stern or bow
float slowly
dripping water

the only sound.
Iridescent sun
blurs the horizon,
we row sunward

through clouds.
Each stroke moves us
to the unseen
out there—waiting.

Passing October

Past midnight cold pierces my pores.

Stars hang like magnets purging dark.

Tiredness overtakes coffee and bourbon.

Stand, change in wavering light

peel off damp layers
bare flesh bristles
smoke composes.

Hobble into longjohns, a fleece,
dry wool socks.

Rake dull coals into a harmless pile.

Bend beneath tent poles,

zip into familiar longings
recoil in a worn sleeping bag.

Lie hushed in stolid dark

decaying oak and cedar
stale scent of myself.

The Weight of Your Loss

    Something cruel
in not saying goodbye

    fog on mountains,
drizzle on windshield, a buzzard
between covered peaks dark
and beautiful from this distance floats
invisible current, a secret passage
as close as imagination above leafless timber
dripping gray

    just about everyone deserves
goodbye eye to eye—a mirror
for the sake of conscience

    don't ambush me by stealing
away in the dark leaving me to carry
the weight of your loss

Song of the Loon

I hear you
tonight
are you lonely

too? I hear
you singing
darkness

across water.
I hear your
deep song

consoling
calling
to mystery

quelling
disappointment.
Night-song

will not
let me sleep
until I feel

your sad tune
echo
my restless mood.

Bless me
bless my wilderness
within.

Algonquin Park

Sitting on a rocky island
no bigger than an efficiency apartment
I face crisp, west breeze.

Waves splash my feet,
an occasional energetic one reaches my thighs
but I do not move.

I am silent on this pile of rock
against the dark surrounding deep, perched
on this unmapped anomaly—a stage prop
midst the curtain of blue-green wilderness.

A heron roosts in the tallest of three scraggly pines.
He will return at sundown to fish after I have taken
all the goggle-eye I want from his water,
drawing them out of their jagged subterranean existence.

A wary loon observes from safe distance
though she tends her own business.
Remember midnight loon cries.
Their daytime demeanor belies haunted voices.
Welcome the lonesome sound.

Immense forest enchants me.
I sit alone, await sunset and consider
how I came to be on this rock.

The Art of Small Things

Any fool can start a big fire
but an artist
manages a small fire

keeps a steady flame
hot enough
to cook with consistency

yet small enough
to avoid burning the cook
or meal.

The art of small things
draws us
to intimate flames

but always warning:
not too close
not too close.

Algonquin Thunder

Circle campfire.

All hands gather wood
take turns poking air holes
stir coals, add sticks.

Thunder roars,
a behemoth belching victims.

Huddle close like lovers

embrace fire
kindle conversation
corral loose thoughts.

Thunder roars,
that giant raging in outer darkness.

We cannot compete with such force.

Tighten the circle, focus
on hypnotic flames
drawing us in to safety.

Thunder—moving now
sounding less now—monster
reclining
     scratching
          giggling.

After the Storm

I
A radiant quarter moon
slices northwestern sky.

A band of indigo clouds
forms the bottom third of sky.

Lighter, fluffy clouds aligning
the top third—drift above.

In the middle a bold clear band
of nothing hosts the moon.

II
Campsites are dark. Folks
are tucked tight, quiet—no fires

no loon calls, no wolves
just waves, eerily passive

after the storm, tapping rocks
tapping, menacing tapping

tapping—like jeering
at the wounded after a fight.

III
Witness a place before
humans—island silhouettes

scattered, darkly visible
echoing the unknown.

Twilight

In twilight
questions seem cruel
wound

but clarify.
Hope dissipates,
nature

looms harsh.
Answer only
in parts

glance
sideways at truth
shrink

from delusion
fear
what will not be

parsed,
unknown particulars
hiding

in midday
brightness, disguised
in contradictions.

But twilight
questions, slants
persists.

On Land

Meditation and water
are wedded forever
　　　—Ishmael in Moby Dick

We think we know on dry land.
Hard earth tricks us—dusty cracks
and stubborn rocks seem eternal

but slip into a canoe at dusk
float among lilies in a Canadian lake
drift with the Pacific tide
or sit by unmarked Ozark springs
rising through rocks

find the glory of *not* knowing,
simple assurance of being
part of the whole.

Seeing the Sea

She cried
and I knew the sea
meant more to her
than surf.

She rides
waves back to childhood
across endless
blue miles.

She knows
all water is connected,
she and the sea
are one.

Before Sunrise

Gray water shines
at dawn like November frost
on a hayfield.

The sun's colors
have yet to blossom,
faint hues flecking
the bay can fool
even old, wise fishermen.

      Flex the rod
      release tense line
      feel the friction

and suppose this is all
I need in life—this,
mullet-chasing mackerel
and regal columns
of pelicans flying low.

Crystal Beach

Sunrise on crystal beach:
Turbulent waves slap me
into submission, exploit
my inability to resist
seductive water.

     See birds
     feel wind
     pick up shells

look for just the right ones

     form matters
     taste governs desire.

Between waves, between
counter-waves, the tide
pushes and pulls my thoughts.

Sandpipers approach,
retreat, re-approach

     I keep thinking loneliness

will give way to meaning,
knowing it might not
but knowing that *that* absence
is presence, and
its own reason for being.

Gull

A gull approaches
as we sit under a palm
by a rented condo.

Every meal he waits,
conditioned by idle tourists
who drop him crumbs.

I notice personality in him,
mannerisms, character.
Let's name him Pete

I say one morning
between sips of coffee.
You are Pete I declare.

Hello Pete
chirps my companion
but Pete smirks

implores us
to consider how many times
he's been named

by vacationers
lounging on this veranda
who mistake

a visit for home
who assume dominion
over Pete

who name gulls
but fail to understand
gulls naming us.

Flounder

Waist-deep in the bay
cast for the sea's bounty

> sunburst
> splashing shrimp

egrets, pelicans take over
tiny islands—rising tide.

I fish a fine flounder
into my net, prop my rod
under my arm, unhook
our evening meal

> she stands beside me
> I string the fish

she takes the stringer
tows the fish

> toward the truck
> toward the ice chest

dark hair curling in breeze
body swaying in time

and for a time
know the dream
that makes a man

Tenderness

A dark-skinned lady curves, whirls
tip-toes on soft sand

bare feet celebrate
discovery of sensuous surf

candy red top hangs loose
above white shorts.

Her hair is up exposing
her strong neck, she glances

over her shoulder at the foaming sea
aware she is being watched

but she's no exhibitionist.

She smiles a self-conscious smile
spins, settles in soft sand

just the way she feels it
just the way he wants it

her husband brings his camera close.
She freezes before blinding flash

then looks to see what image
they've found, what beauty she reflects.

Walk away, unending waves
caress shore with tenderness
I have rarely seen.

Fishing

Wading two hundred yards
from shore at low tide
casting for speckled trout
in silver morning

three porpoise
circle us—fishing
their graceful appearance
belies fierce appetites

our rods raised
in tribute.

North Jetty

At sundown new water
chops the bay
against pink granite.

*If you walk far enough
you come to the curve
in the world, then
look back on yourself*

A lighthouse is now
nothing but relic.

Walk blocks of granite
take air in stride
ponder that shadowy lighthouse

*You must change with time
or be consigned to dust*

but shifting sun shines
other rays as well:

*some things are just the way
they will be
regardless of time,
irrespective of those who
do not see, those
who need no particular light.*

Quicken the pace
wonder how this granite
fell into place,
how the pieces remain
What cavern is their source?

Something introduced
seems natural
if left alone long enough

to break the sea
the sea that would swallow us
if we gave it room
if we left it alone.

Pink egrets land bayside,
a plume-necked bird hunts
alone—a happy family
catching crabs wave.

Return, circle
toward home
thinking of sundown
and that dark lighthouse.

Night Fisherman

He prefers to fish
at night alone—something
in the breeze draws
him, compels him
like a crab, to come

out to darkening surf
where he feels his way
shuffling in sand
estimating sounds in
the waves, this dialogue

with darkness—sundown
beckons. By now he has
caught bait, casting a throw
net and returning line hand
over hand, then sorting

shrimp, mullet. By now
he has greased his reels,
traced the lines with wise-
nerved fingertips—years
of line, years of feel.

He limps, one shoulder
a bit lower, carries a five-
gallon bucket, net, gaff,
two modest rods. He takes
only what the sea gives

but still he must be good
at the getting—old instinct
and stubborn will. He
finds the right place
(always the right place)

sets his gear, attending duty
like a priest preparing
elements of communion,
and like a lone priest
answers only to ritual

under glances of heaven.
He waits the grace of the sea,
alone. Like so many nights
before, soon he will be joined
by bait splashing in gentle

surf, the waning moon, far-off
stars. He sits through black
night hearing his life-song
sung back to him in lonely
and satisfying pitch.

Galveston

At night the sea stalks
romantics who say pleasure
is the softness of sand—
leaning close to hear
in constant wind.

One side of the strip
is man's effort—
white, glaring lights—
the debt we accrue
unto ourselves.

But across the street
waves curl into white foam
laughing at a species
that forgets the glory
of a guiding moon.

Salt

Preserve me
even as you destroy me.

Find hope
in the belly of pain.

The salty sea
soothes, irritates

like a wayfaring brother
lost in strife

with no way
to make him see as I see

like crabs
grabbing false meat

floundering in a net
begging salt.

Save us
from the tide of ourselves.

Scar

Fishing the jetties
she tried to help
slipped on granite
sliced her leg.

She refused help
which I admired
at the time.

The wound closed
tried to heal
but left a scar.

Sometimes
she looks at it
remembering the fall.

Sometimes
we touch, understand
forgive.

But too often
she blames, refuses
help and wounds
never heal.

Tybee Island Sand

Whiteness sprinkles, bathes
calloused feet

    sloshing to surf
    in summer wind.

Twilight keeps you aloft.
Midnight gales hide the moon.

The morning sweep
across my unshaven face

    promises
    but hope

seems just another empty shell
tumbling in endless tide.

Storm on the Waterfront

Gray clouds billow in slow
random order until gray sky
and gray sea loom the same.

Sporadic rain-bursts charm me.

Thunder puts me in my place,
reminds me that I've yet to master
anything so primal as weather.

Beneath thatched grass awning
wind swirls around masts
of docked sailboats, waves build.
Life's currents swell unchecked.

Like any recovering fool

I acknowledge my vulnerability,
applaud my mute
and relative association with aberrant
and familiar wind.

Mustang Island

At 4:30am dark wind
slows, my tent slacks.

From my sleeping bag
I see a quartermoon glow
across black water

and understand
the four most important words
of human history:
Let there be light.

Transience

Motion surrounds me:

Four-wheelers, jet skis, surfers and pickups
filled with bikinied girls and shirtless boys
drinking beer cruise up and down the beach
in constant parade of noisy energy.

Children scurry like gulls in and out of waves.
Fathers hoist kites on wind. Joggers hustle by.
Couples stroll at water's edge making love
to moist sand with their toes.

On the horizon ships line up like pelicans
to deport one by one.

I sit on a mat overwhelmed.

Endless waves approach my feet—then retreat,
like fleeting thoughts playing keep-away
with the elusive sandbar upon which I sit, upon
which a thing called civilization is temporarily settled.

Wind invades and I think I want something
that does not move, one thing I can cling to
in a changing world.

I fear knowing—a cloud in endless
horizon, a wave splashing sand—pretend this beach
is permanent, ignore the truth that we
have already been changed.

Margaritas and Redfish

I

She should have had more sense
than to fall in love with a fisherman.

She knows he knows hooks,
knows how to hold slippery fish
knows quiet dark hours
the web of net, the touch of line.

Waters always move
but she would not flow with them.

He reads sunrise on a morning stream
sunset on the delta coast.

It's all one—this he knows
this she tries to forget.

II

Some nights I just feel like driving
and never stopping.
Interstate 35 rarely opens like the Red Sea.
Moses must have known something strange was up.
What happened to the fish, Moses?

Austin radio will take me to Waco.
At Waco I'll find some station until Fort Worth
to Oklahoma City—tonight
I may wind up in Canada.

Driving under a rustler's moon
the friendly dark accepts my searching mood
echoes my empty words:
It's not bitterness;
It's just that some things don't make sense.

Cheer up, things could be worse.
Sure enough, I cheered up
and things got worse.

This night driving
is like night fishing—you wonder
how your lines will return.

III
Margaritas and Redfish make fine dining.
A band plays in the next room—
CCR, Stones, ZZ Top, Orbison—
all the standards.

Raise a glass to the music
smile at the pretty lady
notice her eyes dancing
as she sings along.

Taste blackened redfish
wild rice and white wine
think of a fisherman
how life would be without him
how some lonely leathered man on the gulf
tends his morning nets
much the same as you

   beneath a twinning sun
      a twinning sun.

To the Desert

She would not come with me
to the desert.

She wanted the masses
where thoughts are muddled
where words are lost.

She would not come with me
to the desert

where nothing is crowded
where nothing is wasted
where nothing is everything.

Balloons above Albuquerque

Saturday morning sky
fills with balloons
floating across town
past the Sandias.

It's cold up there
19 degrees down here
but Saturday sun
calls and they rise

in crowded baskets
beneath fiery engines
cruise above sleepy streets
and empty buildings.

Gliding thin air
bright colors
announce the sensation
above us, above those

who look up and think
about metaphors
of flight suspending
gravity and pain.

Sunrise

Tabernacle in the cusp of sunrise, blessed

    knowing
           enduring
                ignoring

Britney and punk managers of mediocre pancake
houses bums begging streets oblivious to desire
melding way past hope of meaning or sunrise.

East is the way to look
after Catholic bells gong in Old Town
at Saturday vespers, after the fury
of strippers clothe themselves
to forget coming days.

Blue-black outlines of mountains
invoke sacrifice, redemption
and paltry attempts to forgive.

Artificial rapture leaves me craving the unseen
clinging to a mother's prayers—solitary
without media, absent fanfare—simple

like sun and mountain
and sky—the everlasting sky.

Timberline

I've come to these mountains
to grieve, breathe
fade above timberline
high above domestic claims.

Up here rocks burnished
by wind, melting snow
unfiltered sun color
the lake before me.

Up here lightning strikes
from glaucous clouds
stalk the vastness
pierce even hardest peaks.

I consider my next move
realize I could wait too long
(but unsure when that would be)
not wanting to miss the splendid event.

Tonight I'll sleep below alpine flowers
in a grove of birch. Hear
night settle, indulge
in simple breath.

Purple Song

On the purple side of the mountain
the other side of sundown
I find myself looking
across quiescent bunchgrass
scattered boulders
dark-shadowed juniper
white-tipped yucca dotting
the valley below.

In luminous, arid dark-fall
I know what matters
is to be still, to remember
that I am not alone—
I am countless intricacies
continuously intersecting—
birthed in temporary flight
resting now in purple shadows.

Caprock Canyon

In mid-March only juniper
is green, prickly pear, some
yucca, the underside of sage.
The rest holds drab winter
hues peppered along red rims

and rusty dirt of my camp.
Scrub brush, thorns, tiny buds
of mesquite poised to break forth
in splendor when time is right
when sufficient warmth makes

the desert bloom overnight
in understated spectacle.
My tent is pitched, southwest
winds slow, north clouds approach.
Rain or snow will fall by morning.

I may not see stars tonight,
but they burn above me.
Quiet takes over campfires
dotted along this valley
dark nature will have its way.

The peace of nightsky prevails
with pinion-smoke—settle
down aware—praise the desert
soul with somber hymns
and sleep the daybirds know.

Fishing Creede Colorado

For all of us
it's simply a matter of time.

My passion is a flyrod
and wild-streaming cutthroats—
yours may be something else

      but what is true
      for me is true for you:

up on the divide
mule deer and bighorn sheep
among aspen and spruce
spring but for a season.

The lore of this place
informs us all: gunslingers
can never retire.

Even good killings
from our shadowy pasts

fade into blurry youth—
time that seems
never to have been.

43

Mount Scott

Crawl through granite and cedar
where wind and sun bake clean.
Sit where silence rules wind,
a road three thousand feet below,
spotted blue lakes beyond.

Look out to flatland extending
as far as imagination carries
yet that distance is no farther
than the hope and fear
we allow inside our hearts.

When life is battled and bottled
take your bruises to the mountain,
rest in cedar shade until the color
of granite pinkens your gills,
know the heart will soon follow.

A Yesterday or Two

Rowing backward across a captious lake
like a crawdad, backing again to a place
we left, seems so long ago now
but really was only a yesterday or two
when we laughed our way through fallen
leaves skimming the surface,
sunfish poised just below them.

If I row enough I will back through time
until I realize that fish below water
have the same concern as you and I—
how to find satisfaction without giving yourself
away, suspended between then and now
but with one critical difference:
really, what do sunfish know?

Mud Turtle

Sloshing through grassy sandstone
along a lake shore I pause,
look through turbid drizzle
sense I belong beyond knowing,
breathe slow, exhaling
until I am still enough to hear
whispers of uncertain wind.

He rises out of murky water
thinking he is alone before
noticing me and disappearing
as quickly as he appeared,
dissipating ripples
the only evidence of his presence
that we in fact saw each other.

Water covers his re-entry and I
think maybe I should envy turtles,
their ability to rise and fall
unnoticed, belonging to places
where humans are *merely* visitors
to be reminded of unions
visceral and misunderstood.

Storm on a Mountain Ridge

Blue clouds turn even bluer.
The happy feel of solitude
ducks its head into itself

like turtles sucking fear.
I find space within myself
to hold somewhat at peace

the lies we know remain
      wild wind blows
      pressure falls

      hard rain jabs.
I ball myself in fortitude,
try to not be tense, so high

so close to God so full of gall,
sense blackjacks bending taut,
think of birds tucked

somehow, somewhere, feel
common plight and wish
for feathers half so fierce.

On a Mountain in Solitude

On a mountain in solitude
my want of love bounces
off iron rocks, dreams
wisping in slight air.

When you've given everything
more than once you wonder
what may be left, what feelings
could matter anymore

whether a squirrel nest atop
a white oak might not suffice.
Would advice from a cranky raven
be to find soul here among limbs

or to take a path that always
returns down the hill?

Lonely Days

When lust of betrayal burns
fire orange—a hunter slicing fields
eyes seared for any movement
in bunchgrass or wheat stalks
or plum thicket and ragweed
lining fence rows

follow bent creosote poles thinly
connected to rusting, sagging wire, know
only the land is beyond reproach

thank the wind for taking your pain
aloft—even if at times it swirls back your way.

Blue Texas Guitar

I sense sound
aggressive, tainted—
I can do nothing
but hear it hard.

Jugular rhythm—
blood-spilled, bare
on backroads
where kingsome drifters

seek refuge
from working soil,
bridle their mind
bleeding until death

one drop at a time.
Slow-hearted
angular weeds
piercing the ditches

undeniable, proud.
Like mockingbirds flitting
round your back door
atone for all things

once out of tune—
filling voids
soaring, clamoring
for more, and then some.

Thunder in the Morning

Of all the sounds that frame my hearing
nothing stirs me like thunder in the morning
sends me to a preternatural state of hope
compensates in ways I don't expect,
a gift from a cosmos I can only imagine.

I remember lilies around the walnut tree
the last thing I saw before sleep.
I hear birds singing through raindrops,
the swoop of wind through April leaves.

The world I manage is often parched,
athirst with wrongheaded desire,
dusty souls in need of a good stirring.

Often

Often I open the door to let in
the sound of rain tapping
along with a Brahm's symphony
or the Allman Brothers—often
my pen cannot keep pace
with the dropping water
or the chilling violins or
the tragic guitars—often
I remind myself that rain,
like music, like a pen moving
on paper, is what the world
needs most. It could be
that the thunder outside
is no match for the singing birds
at rainy dawn. It could be
that the collection of their voices
is a light that brings us home.

An Ozark Place

Swallows dive for unsuspecting mayflies
suspended above a creek where
transparent water ripples over a gravel
matrix combining endless shapes
and sizes and densities into a bed
gentle enough to sleep on.

Thunder resonates through defining bluffs
marking this hidden spot few people
ever see—a wilderness apart—a world
unto its own.

Walk lightly—don't interrupt—I am
a privileged guest, witness to things
defying explanation, flourishing without me.

Up Here

Rapids below
seem faster, whiter
move with strange silence
as tomorrow
pushes today.

Up here, alone
hear whooshing wings
wild turkeys rising
to roost on bent limbs
facing sunset.

Up here, distance
blurs memories
one by one—
things so long ago
so far below.

Winter Rain

Sadness in the air drips
on tin, splatters leaves
plinks pond water.

A creek connects
left-over leaves, bare
limbs, sparse yellow grass.

In the trees a solitary cabin:

> candles lit
> a lady sweeps
> somebody stirs supper

listen, listen to winter rain.
Sadness falls somewhere
but not here—not tonight.

Curtain call

When others are still in bed
I will be loading my gear
looking through sleepy eyes
for the key to my old truck,
a kayak on top tied down
the night before.

While others sleep I will drive
through morning dark smelling grass
and honeysuckle blow
through open windows, coffee
bouncing in a travel cup—
the humming tires.

With the early streaks of light
I will be standing waist-deep
in a stream, toes curling
on slippery rocks, stubby
fingers following flyline
in dark water.

I will hear life splashing close
and think how lucky I am
to be alone on stage
at the last curtain of night—
fool player performing lines
few care to hear.

At Mountain Fork River

From arcane depths jagged
boulders break the current,
an upheaval still felt.

At dusk a fisherman arcs
through hovering mist, each

cast slices damp air, filets
the backbone of memory.

On dark shore under gothic
oak and pine, a charred pot

half-filled with stale coffee
sits by a fire pit
as flames become ash.

Stars

for Debbie Hada Moore

Everything we know
is in the past, stars
burning out above

us, twittering spots
of light fall through time
making the darkness

livable. Better
to know old ways, the
former loves, other

lives in retrospect.
Then again, how could
one know anything

before it fell, white
gas filling space, the
void of a moment?

Meteor

I don't think I'll ever forget you
streaking through the black 5 am sky,
fierce light penetrating darkness, a long
luminous tail glowing, hanging
like a marathon in empty atmosphere
leaving me breathless.

I guess now I would say that you
were nothing but random—I just happened
to see you burning toward nothing,
rogue fireball mistaken for glory, but then
I contemplated—anticipated
what this exhilarating omen might mean.

Now I wonder why something
out of the ordinary should be meaningful.

Sitting in the cold cab of my pickup
that morning, the cold mocking my acute
sense of betrayal, I lean forward, rest
my chin on the brittle steering wheel, look
through a frosty window, shudder
and believe what I want to believe.

Old Loves

They blend like rivers:

At the confluence of Crooked Creek
    and White River on a hot day, cold
    water and new thoughts combine
    like rivers, old love slipping over rocks,
    a fish skeleton lying off-current in shallows,
    minnows and sunfish nibbling bones.

A dead, leafless sycamore leans over
    water like a spear from a monstrous god
    planted in the heart of a hillside, green
    hardwoods surrounding.

Hear ripples and a male cardinal, dip the oar
    and push away downstream, the canoe
    bottom scraping gravel, my sleeves uprolled
    bearing an honest tan.

Paddle toward sunset, that lonely
    time when I will locate my truck, load up
    and head for some home. No one wants
    to be alone when the sun goes down.

We decide our access points, when
    and where to put in, when and where
    to get out.

Getting in and out:

    Two distinct but similar acts, both
    capable of confusion, dangerous yet
    essential, welcomed or not.

Where Crooked Creek joins White River
ponder new meanings to old questions.
Maybe questions, not answers, serve purpose.

When we ask the right questions the right
way at the right time, convergence occurs
the way water intersects water, the way
it lays in the discovery of our concatenated universe.

Shade is not easy to find:

But cool water on my feet and legs
provides a balance between caution
and fearless adventure, without which
no river can be known.

Hands don't betray these moments.
These last strokes will be the longest, heavy
in the corporeal, falling sun evocative
in contemplation and beautiful in the leaving.

Pennington Creek in November

Notice my footprints in sandy-gravel
lost too soon in the current,
the same current I need to float

line and fly into a dark eddy
beside a broken log, stuck
for a bit, in the same settled sand.

Rod flexed, line searching overhead,
creep, try to avoid ripples, do not
alert hunted fish. The stream

passes. Dead leaves and twigs float
by—scant signs of decay pass
my vain attempts to hold bliss.

Hold the corked handle of a favorite
flyrod, grip delusions hoping to touch
meaning without disturbing current.

Beautiful November haunts, speaks
with silence: The bliss of a moment
overtaken by every passing element

reminds of what too often I
forget—the life I seek is cherished
in the dying around, within.

A Creek No One Knows

This coldest night of my life,
colder than heaven's blue
stretches toward universes
that can only be numbered.

Sometimes we earthy folks
put up wire or maybe board
to prevent Infinity
from turning us to crystal.

Tonight down by a creek
no one knows an old doe
watches the lungs of her weaker
twin collapse and harden.

Beneath brutal stars soft flesh
quickly stiffens to something
not to be gathered, but for eyes
glassy, enduring.

Can you hear water trickling
like a hunter stalking prey
interrupting the Absolute
with the terror of footsteps?

Between Rain

Light a pot of coffee
beneath a lean-to tarp
sort through packs
think dully of breakfast
trying to start a morning.

Sniff soggy air, rain
blows again. Crawl
into the tent, fall
on hard ground against
soft coils of your body.

Conspiring Rain

Morning rain wakens me
to sounds I don't fully know.
I've been rhythmed in my sleep
and now I wish you were here
in my bed, I think, and roll
over desiring other times when
you would have enjoyed this
dreamy state of mind that
sensuous rain brings, merging
longing with memory.

Instead I fear betrayal
of my senses and question
the motive of seductive
rain, hoping it is not part
of a bigger set up in which
little plots I routinely face
are aligning beyond my control,
despotic rain drops dripping
with deception, conspiring
all around me.

Yellow Cottonwoods

There's heartache in these lines
cracking through once-hard ground
crumbling to dust.

Sadness drifts here
under yellow cottonwoods
where old men sit
in a distorted circle—a parlor
for the ornery and rejected
where a can of beer
accompanies a worn story
told with fading bravado
swallowing fear in quick gulps.

These grains of river sand
drying in wind sift
through time, pile around toes
of shuffling boots, legs
dangling off a tailgate
or sitting awry in a chair
whose fabric is stretched
past the point of brittle.

Sand Plums on the Canadian River

He walks the lesser part of day
along the river's path slipping
through shifting sand, eyes
pierced for plumpest, ripest

picks. His face is course, his
fingers hard, he squints away
the western sun—a pail of plums
half full, meadowlarks in flight.

Stars above Oklahoma

If you look up in black night
past cottonwood leaves
through the prairie wind
you will find stars above Oklahoma,
fiery gas-stones flinging fierce
glory you could not have foreseen,
glowing that overwhelms, feels
eternal. You grow small and alone
but try to remember those who
traveled this prairie before you,
mystic nomads who also navigated
the dark wind beneath a haunting
array of arrow-tipped light piercing
the very organ of being.

The Coyote in All of Us

A moon shivers in feral sky.
The cries of coyotes echo
in the void, pierce the silence

between a canyon and forever.
Shrill voices slice the dark
and the light in chilling fragments,

remind me of the pain
I thought I had forgotten,
the betrayal of prairie moon.

If I told you my grandpa
as a young man
had a coyote for a pet

you might not believe me
but I have an old, sepia photo
of a young man crouching

beside a wild dog, each
wary of the other, both
seem surprised to be so close.

I have also been told
grandpa used to run down
jackrabbits on foot.

This wild night,
this wild night
yammering beneath timeless stars

I shudder to contemplate
that which came before me
the coyote in all of us.

In the Stillness of This Place

a hundred birds cackle, sing, call,
serenade the silence—trees standing
windless, blades of grass unbending,
creek water crawling over silt
on limestone—and I become aware
of the rare vision a mother dog knows
straddling her bug-ridden pup biting
flesh til it bleeds, biting then licking
until the blood clots, until the pain
recedes—licking her wounds, a primal
cure tender mongrels know so well

Residue

Swallows flitter
beneath gray-white clouds

Raindrops drip
down catalpa leaves

Blue patches
dot the western sky

Husk-less walnuts
blacken a walkway

Moments rise
then fade to goodness

Rituals at Dusk

A cigar at sundown after supper
sipping a glass of rose wine
as the wind settles

a doe lollops in clover
where prairie pentstemon stands
at the edge of a yard

a few birds chase flies
in the calm before whippoorwills
and tree frogs chant darkness full.

These are the days of green
repose, of evening bliss
before summer simmers down.

These are ceremonies you keep:
simple, smoky intercession
savored once again.

Red River Epiphany

I'm standing mid-river below a hundred feet
of concrete that dams a potent stream
flowing from a hidden spring, building
through salty, sandy soil, freely, like love
should be, unhindered passion loosed
like truth, flourishing, nourishing.

Mauve sunset beyond me, water slips
by. I pause my casting, consider that giant
wall holding pent-up water, collecting
on the other side, it's natural course slowed,
its flowing corralled for the moment.

Several hundred miles of water pushes
this obstruction but dams do not have final
say—a river will have its way—flood
gates must be opened.

You no more stopped me
than dams stop rivers.

Everything I Am

Silver water splays a twenty foot wall
of travertine, afternoon shadows lengthen.

Winter has passed since I've returned
to these falls, a cedar trunk hangs gaunt
over splashing water, its green top branches
given over at last to ice

but a bare sycamore and a thick cottonwood
remain above the rapids I have fished so well.

I am lost in the sound of falling water.
I am surrounded with the familiar sense
that I am flowing in the current before me.

I am dripping through canyons I cannot conquer

     these arcane forms
     these wild arrays

shape everything I am.

Mistress

She never fails
to give
more than she takes
seducing me
into her pools,
my flyrod upright
casting aloft.

Water
lapping my legs
I tremble
in pulsating current
drawing me deeper
inside her
luscious self.

Vow

At Longmire Lake a quail
calls a summer evening song,
really a whistle shrilling
in patient rhythm

proud, clear, asserting
his simple scale.
I turn my ear to the wind,
feel the solitary call.

He doesn't sound unhappy.
I imagine
he seeks something
I also want (*you have not*

because you ask not).
Beside choppy waves,
finger line to catch
soft-striking crappies

vow to ask what wild
birds ask—and sense
I may possess it already
just by the asking.

Focus

Sitting on a park bench
facing east at sunset
I look into the mirror lake
before me.

Evening falls unannounced
reflecting the opposite bank,
a pattern emerges on the water:

red and yellow leaves
among brown-green background
under amber clouds.

The image grows
more sharply into focus
the later it gets.

In These Sandy Shores

If the morning comes without you
and the only friends I know
are the pileated, and the wrens
and mockingbirds, if the only sound
is water sloshing between granite
uprisings along cedar-lined shore
it will have been enough.

I cannot know what might have been.
I can only imagine what never was.

But the salty sunrise
along the river blue, the gnats
and flies and late spring humidity
between gusts of dusky breeze
mark me for a time, this time
until the love of earth
buries me in these sandy shores.

www.ingramcontent.com/pod-product-compliance
Lightning Source LLC
Chambersburg PA
CBHW020949090426
42736CB00010B/1337